Elizabeth Cady Stanton

(1815–1902)

by

Martha E. Kendall

illustrated by

Anne R. Knight

for Billie Jensen),
whose Women in U. S. History
class first inspired me to want to learn
even more about Elizabeth Cady Stanton.
thank you!
Marty Kendall
august, 1987

Heart of the Lakes Publishing
Interlaken, New York
1987

Library of Congress Cataloging-in-Publication Data

Kendall, Martha, 1947–
    Elizabeth Cady Stanton,   b. November 12, 1815,   d. October
26, 1902.

    Summary: A biography of the nineteenth-century pioneer
in the struggle for women's rights.
    1. Stanton, Elizabeth Cady, 1815–1902.   2. Feminists –
United States – Biography – Juvenile literature.   [1. Stanton,
Elizabeth Cady, 1815–1902.   2. Feminists]   I. Title.
HQ1413.S67K46 1987   324.6'23'.0924 [B] [92]   86-7569
ISBN: 0-932334-29-6

ISBN: 0-932334-29-6
Manufactured in the United States of America

A *quality* publication from
Heart of the Lakes Publishing
Interlaken, New York 14847

Contents

Illustrations

"No, Don't Do That!"

"You must act more like a proper young lady," scolded Mary Dunn. Elizabeth said nothing, but thought to herself, "A proper young lady doesn't get to do very much!" Mary, the strict Scottish nanny, had heard about Elizabeth and her sister's behavior at church that morning, and she told Elizabeth, "Go upstairs and work on your embroidery. You must learn to set a good example for your sister, and to behave like the daughter of a fine family!"

Elizabeth slowly started up the steps, thinking about what had happened at church. She, her sister Margaret, and Peter, the black man who had cared for the many Cady children for nearly twenty years, had entered just as the service was about to begin. The usher led Elizabeth and Margaret to the front pew where the important families sat, but he waved to Peter, because he was black, to sit at the back of the church.

Elizabeth and Margaret darted by the usher. They paid no attention when he said angrily, "No, don't do that!" and they sat down next to Peter in the back row.

The congregation was shocked. Children of Daniel Cady, the most important man in Johnstown, were sitting alongside a black servant!

The Cady children loved Peter. After all, he took them wading in the creek, and exploring in the orchard. They didn't care if his skin was black!

When Elizabeth reached the top of the stairs and entered her room, she found a huge pile of unfinished embroidery staring at her. Just then, Margaret peeked into the room and whispered, "Elizabeth, let's go over to the mill pond. All our friends will be waiting for us!"

They quietly slipped out the back door, ran and got Peter, and sure enough, found half a dozen girls already playing along the shore of the pond when they arrived.

Feeling brave after standing up to the usher in church that morning, Elizabeth said, "Today I shall man the raft. I'll navigate." She had often seen the big boys poling the rafts

5

around the pond, and surely she could do it too. She and Margaret leapt onto a raft, Elizabeth grabbed a long pole, and out they floated.

"Push with the pole," yelled Peter from shore.

Elizabeth tried and tried to lift the pole, but it was too heavy for her. The raft just drifted on its own, carrying its two small passengers. Before long, the girls realized where the gentle current was taking them—toward the dam!

"Sit down," Elizabeth yelled to the terrified Margaret. The raft picked up speed as it neared the dam, and the water rushed about them. "Hold tight!" Elizabeth commanded. They both gripped the sides hard, and over the dam they went.

Peter jumped into the water. The raft was still right side up, the girls clinging to it. Pushing his way across the current, he managed to catch the raft and its young crew in the stream below.

"Peter, oh Peter, thank you!" they cried as he pulled them safely to shore. Calling goodbye to their friends, Elizabeth, Margaret and their rescuer, all of them dripping wet, headed for home. This time they were in luck, and they succeeded in avoiding Mary Dunn's watchful eyes. She thought Elizabeth and Margaret had spent the afternoon quietly embroidering up in their rooms.

Daniel Cady's law office was attached to the Cady home, and sometimes when Elizabeth's temper went beyond Mary Dunn's patience, Elizabeth was sent to her father. If he was busy, she was to sit in the corner, not utter a word, and listen while he advised the people who came to see him.

There in his office, Elizabeth learned that the laws of New York State in the 1820s could be very harsh for the men who broke them. But she also learned that for women, the laws could be very harsh when they were obeyed!

One afternoon Mary Dunn put her hands on her hips and looked despairingly at Elizabeth. She said, "It is impossible to get you to embroider slowly and neatly as a proper young lady should. Go down to your father!"

Elizabeth slowly entered her father's big office, but before she had to explain why Mary had sent her there, she was relieved to hear a knock on the door. Flora Campbell walked

in. Elizabeth was surprised to see the neighbor coming to the law office. Usually she went to the back door bringing fresh vegetables from her garden to share with the Cady family. Elizabeth listened closely as Mrs. Campbell told her story.

"Mr. Cady, when my father passed away many years ago, he left me the old family home. When I married, we stayed there. Now, as you know, my dear husband has died."

"Yes, I know, Mrs. Campbell. You have my sympathy. He was a good man," said Mr. Cady, and Elizabeth saw the widow's eyes fill with tears.

"But now," Mrs. Campbell went on, "Jock, my husband's son by his first marriage, has started drinking, has spent almost every penny of our savings, and told me I have to get out of the house, that it's his now. Tell me that can't be true!"

After a long pause, Mr. Cady said, "The laws are in the books." He pointed to the many volumes that lined his shelves. "The woman's property becomes her husband's when she marries. If her husband dies, the property goes to his legal heir. In this case, that's his son Jock. There's nothing I can do. I'm sorry."

Elizabeth knew she was not supposed to speak when a client was present, but she could not remain silent. "But why, Father? Why do the laws say that?"

Mrs. Campbell, who was about to leave the office, paused to hear the answer.

Judge Cady explained. "A married woman is considered an extension of her husband. Legally, husband and wife are one. The law expects the husband to control and protect all property, earnings and children. If he decides to will a house to his son, that is his right."

Mrs. Campbell, who had cheerfully visited the Cadys many times before, left the house this time looking sad and desperate. Now she had no husband, no money left, and no home.

Elizabeth's heart cried out to her. Those laws must be wrong! She decided that she would take the scissors and cut those mean laws out of her father's books.

But before Elizabeth had a chance to get away from Mary Dunn long enough to do just that, Mr. Cady explained to her that the laws were made by men in the New York State

Legislature. He said, "When you are grown up, and able to prepare a speech, you must go to Albany and talk to the legislators."

Mr. Cady succeeded in preventing his little daughter from cutting up his law books, but he did not know that his advice that day would set in motion her determination to change laws that were unfair, even though women at that time weren't even allowed to vote, much less to make laws!

"You Should Have Been a Boy!"

"Be quiet," hushed Tryphena, the oldest Cady daughter, looking angrily at the eleven-year-old Elizabeth. "Eleazer may be sleeping."

Elizabeth instantly stopped talking. Her only brother had just graduated from Union College, but he had come home gravely ill. Mr. Cady walked slowly down the hall and entered the sick room.

"I've never seen him look so sad," thought Elizabeth. "Surely I can help."

But Eleazer's health got worse, and within a week, he died.

Mr. Cady was overcome with grief, and he sat staring at the coffin of his only son. Elizabeth climbed onto his lap. Mr. Cady sighed deeply, and without looking away from Eleazer, he said, "Oh, my daughter, I wish you were a boy!"

Elizabeth threw her arms around her father and promised, "I will try to be all my brother was."

All the next day she thought hard about what boys could do and what girls could do. She knew many adults liked boys more. Elizabeth remembered back to the cold January morning when her youngest sister Kate was born. People had said, "What a pity it is she's a girl."

Elizabeth could never be a boy, but somehow she wanted to make her father happy again. Maybe she could be as good as a boy!

First, boys were supposed to be good at education. So early the next morning Elizabeth went to see Reverend Simon Hosack, a kind neighbor who knew Greek from his student days. Every morning Elizabeth studied a new section of his grammar book, and she learned fast. Dr. Hosack told Mr. Cady, "Elizabeth has a very fine mind." Mr. Cady nodded absently, and said nothing. His thoughts were still on his buried son.

"Boys do more than learn Greek," said Elizabeth, so she set out to learn to manage horses as they did. After much prodding, she finally convinced Peter to let her drive the small carriage by herself, and she handled the gentle chestnut gelding well.

"Now I must ride the spirited bay mare," she decided. Every day after her Greek lesson, she climbed up onto the mare and went for long rides. She recited Greek phrases aloud to practice what she'd studied that morning, and her chatter seemed to calm the nervous horse.

One afternoon she tried a new way home. A breeze gave both her and the horse extra energy, and they trotted briskly along the unfamiliar path. Wild blackberries lined the trail, and surprised rabbits jumped out of the way. Elizabeth let the mare break into a gallop, and her dark curly hair streamed out from underneath the edges of her riding cap.

As they rounded a bend, Elizabeth yelled out "Whoa!" A big log had fallen, blocking the trail. But they were going too fast to stop. The mare perked up her ears, Elizabeth gripped tight, and they sailed over the log.

Her Greek momentarily forgotten, Elizabeth said aloud to the mare, "Now that was as good as a boy!"

When they came to a thick hedgerow bordering Reverend Hosack's meadow, Elizabeth clucked to the mare and they jumped it easily. And instead of riding around the ditch by the Cady barn as she used to do, she guided the mare straight over the ditch in a graceful leap.

That night at dinner Elizabeth told about her new accomplishments on horseback. Mrs. Cady shook her head at Elizabeth's daring. Tryphena and Harriet disapproved of their younger sister's unladylike conduct, but Margaret and little Kate looked enviously at her.

Mr. Cady paid no attention.

Elizabeth's progress in Greek was so remarkable that the teachers at the Johnstown Academy took notice. She was moved up to the advanced class of older boys. Every year the Academy awarded two prizes to the most outstanding students of Greek. At the big assembly when the prizes were given, Elizabeth tried to stay calm.

"No girl has ever won a Greek prize," she thought. "And last week I did misspell two words on my examination." She

eyed the boy in class who had been the best student for the past three years. He towered over Elizabeth, who still didn't stand even five feet tall.

"And now," the Headmaster said, "we shall award the most coveted prizes in the Academy, for the best students of Greek."

"I must smile bravely," Elizabeth said to herself as the tall boy stepped forward to receive the first prize. And then, could it be? Yes, the Headmaster was saying, "And now, the second prize goes to a fine young lady, a truly outstanding student—Elizabeth Smith Cady."

Elizabeth did her best to act like a lady when she walked up to the platform to receive the prize, but all she could think of was running home to show her father.

She didn't stay to hear the congratulations of her friends after the ceremony, but instead hurried across Johnstown. She burst into Mr. Cady's law office and proudly held her Greek prize before him. Now he would see she was as good as a son.

Mr. Cady sighed, kissed her on the forehead, and said, "Ah, you should have been a boy."

One of Eleazer's classmates at Union College, Edward Bayard, became a regular visitor at the Cadys', and before long he and Tryphena were married. For Elizabeth and her sisters, Edward helped to fill the void left by Eleazer. The newlyweds stayed at the Cady home, and soon they were joined by Edward's brother Henry. Both studied law in Mr. Cady's office, for he had just been appointed a judge.

These two young men enjoyed the company of the Judge's daughters, and they shared their lessons and their pranks with the girls. They often teased Elizabeth, for she was the brightest and most ambitious of them all.

One Christmas morning Elizabeth happily showed Edward and Henry her new coral necklace and bracelets. Henry could not resist this chance to make Elizabeth's blue eyes flash with anger, and he said, "Elizabeth, of course you know that if you should ever marry, your husband could take this jewelry and do whatever he wanted with it. He could trade it for cigars and you could watch your presents go up in smoke!" Elizabeth stalked off, holding the necklace and bracelets tight, with the law students chuckling behind her.

In the fall of 1830, the boys from Elizabeth's class at the Academy left Johnstown. "Goodbye, good luck!" she called to her former classmates as they drove away in the stagecoach headed for Union College. Even though Elizabeth was always one of the best students, she could not attend Union. In 1830, no college in America admitted females.

Elizabeth went for a ride on the mare that afternoon and thought about her future in Johnstown. "I, too, deserve more education. I will not sit home and do embroidery and listen to Edward and Henry's mean stories about women!"

That evening she resoundly beat Edward at a game of chess. Then she confronted Judge Cady.

"Father, I can ride horses as well as a boy, I have learned Greek better than most of them, and I can outsmart my opponents in chess at least as often as they do me. You are a Judge now. Can't you find a way for me to attend Union College?"

Judge Cady rubbed his chin. The same expression of grief which he'd had when Eleazer died, once again crossed his face.

"Elizabeth," he said, "you are a young lady now, and you've had enough education. It's time for you to socialize with young men and enjoy dinners and dances. The only thing you still need to learn is how to keep house and prepare fine meals."

Elizabeth was so angry she could not even reply to her father. She stomped out and looked for Edward. When she found him, she said, "It isn't fair! I love school and I am smarter than most of the boys! Father can afford the tuition, but I still can't go to college—because I'm a girl!" And she repeated, "It isn't fair!"

Edward promised Elizabeth he would talk to her father about it. Eventually Judge Cady was persuaded to let Elizabeth have more education, but "at a proper school for girls," he told her. "In January, you may go to Mrs. Willard's Female Seminary in Troy."

An Education at Mrs. Willard's Seminary

"We'll never make it up that hill east of Schenectady!" said the slender woman, nervously adjusting her purse and parcels.

"Harumph," mumbled a rather dignified gentleman seated across the aisle. "This train is a model of Yankee ingenuity."

Overhearing them, a beaming grandmother said, "Why, when I was a child, I never dreamed I'd be able to take a train from Schenectady to Albany and not have to ride that horrible stagecoach. I'm glad it's 1831 and we're in the modern age!"

Elizabeth only half listened to the other passengers. Her mind was filled with questions. "What will Mrs. Willard's school be like? Will I learn there even half of what I could have learned at Union College? How will I get along with the other girls?"

The train jolted, and Elizabeth and her fellow passengers anxiously looked out the windows. The train stopped for a moment, and they heard loud clanking noises and much yelling. Then the train began again, unevenly jerking its way along.

"We've been hooked to the stone-carrying train," said a man who obviously enjoyed knowing everything. "We're being pulled up this hill by another train, loaded with heavy rocks, that's going down the other side."

This simple system finally succeeded in dragging the passenger train up the high hill. They then chugged on to Albany, where Elizabeth boarded a coach for Troy.

"This dormitory looks like the jail back in Johnstown!" she thought as she entered the dreary building. The giggling voices of excited girls welcomed her. About one hundred students attended Mrs. Willard's Seminary, and their main interest seemed to be to try to arrange meetings with any

17

boys who might come into the neighborhood. This, of course, had not been the intention of Mrs. Willard. The girls were to focus on "scholarship, if you please!"

In those days it was not unusual for girls of prosperous families to be sent to "finishing schools" where they were taught social graces and domestic skills to prepare them to become proper wives. Elizabeth's rebellious mind was not about to be "finished," and although she had not been allowed to attend Union College, she did appreciate the progressive offerings at Mrs. Willard's. She liked best the classes which were not even available at any other girls' boarding schools, especially logic, philosophy and composition.

It did not take long for everyone to notice how good a writer Elizabeth was, and one evening a friend in her composition class shyly knocked on her door.

"Have your finished the homework assignment for tomorrow, the one to describe our rooms?" she nervously asked.

"Yes, I just did," answered Elizabeth. "Would you like to see it?"

"Oh, yes, thank you," she answered. "I finished mine, but I don't think it's very good. Would you mind taking a look at it? You're such a good writer."

Flattered, Elizabeth read her friend's paper, which indeed was not very well done. However, to make her feel better, Elizabeth praised it. She said, "Oh, your paper is excellent. Why, it's better than mine!"

"Oh, do you really think so? Then let's trade! Our rooms are all enough alike that no one will ever know." She thanked Elizabeth again and ducked out of the room, leaving Elizabeth caught by her well-intended but false compliment.

When they read their papers aloud in class the next day, the one Elizabeth had written was greeted with delighted laughter and applause. When Elizabeth read her friend's, as if it were her own, only a few people clapped politely.

"Miss Cady, did you write that paper?" the composition teacher asked loudly.

"Y-y-yes," stammered Elizabeth.

"That's odd," said the techer, "because the exact same paper was handed in by another student as well!"

Everyone gasped, and Elizabeth realized her friend must have tricked another girl, too, but had come to Elizabeth hoping to get an even better paper. Her face red with embarrassment, Elizabeth hurried back to her seat. She didn't tell on her friend, but she felt terribly ashamed.

Late that day another knock on her door made Elizabeth jump. It was the composition teacher!

"Elizabeth, I know all the students' handwriting by now. I know the truth. Which composition did you really write?" the teacher asked.

Elizabeth told the whole story.

"If I had not found this out, would you have remained silent about what happened?" the teacher asked.

"Yes," said Elizabeth.

"Really, my child, you have not used your common sense in this matter," said the teacher, shaking her head as she left the room.

When her friend was scolded in front of the class the next day for what she had done, Elizabeth cried for her. Compared to the lesson they had just learned, writing compositions was easy work.

A few weeks later, when she was practicing for her singing class, another girl asked Elizabeth, "Have you heard about the revival?"

Putting the guitar down, Elizabeth said, "No. What revival?"

"Reverend Dr. Charles Finney is going to hold a six-week revival meeting here in Troy. All the girls are going."

When Elizabeth arrived at the first meeting, the hall was already crowded. Dr. Finney was speaking from the pulpit with an enthusiasm and sincerity Elizabeth had never seen in a preacher before. Fascinated, she decided to attend every session.

"Sinners shall be punished, and we are all sinners!" Dr. Finney's big voice boomed. Elizabeth's nerves were on edge. She had disappointed her father by being a girl, she had disobeyed Mary Dunn, she had never embroidered as well as she could have, she had been caught trading compositions. "My list of sins is endless!" she cried.

Nightmares awakened her, and visions of lost souls haunted her dreams. Guilt and worries constantly distracted her. When the school year ended and Elizabeth returned to Johnstown, the Cadys could not believe the change in their daughter.

"Elizabeth is terrified of the devil!" said Mrs. Cady. "What happened to her carefree, cheerful personality? I want the old Elizabeth back, even if she stirs up mischief as she used to!"

"A trip, away from fears of religion—that will cure her," said Judge Cady. So he decided to take Elizabeth, Tryphena and her husband Edward to Niagara Falls. "We shall see the sights and discuss everything the world has to offer, except the punishment of the devil!" the Judge announced.

That glorious June, Elizabeth's mind broke free of Dr. Finney's gloomy pronouncements. Edward talked to her about reason and logic, and he gave her books about new scientific ideas. The cloud lifted from Elizabeth's face and her bright blue eyes sparkled once again.

Learning From a Slave Girl

T he two remaining years at Mrs. Willard's passed quickly, and after Elizabeth graduated, she became a popular young lady with Johnstown's men looking for a bride. The law students loved to flirt with the Judge's daughter.

One in particular liked to tease Elizabeth, especially about women's supposed inferiority to men. One day, having heard enough from him, Elizabeth asked Peter to saddle "Old Boney," the roughest, meanest and most difficult horse in the stable. Peter, friend as always, did as she asked and handed the horse over to the young man. Elizabeth mounted her favorite mare and off she galloped.

"Whoa, wait up!" the student called. "I can't make this unruly beast mind me!"

Elizabeth pretended not to hear, and she stayed just far enough ahead of him that he could not catch her, but neither could he turn around and go back without her seeing him give up.

When the ride was over, the student mumbled as he gave the horse back to Peter, "Oh, my legs hurt, my hands are sore, my back aches." He hobbled slowly back to his hotel.

Elizabeth winked at Peter and hid a smile as she strolled from the stable. "Hopefully this will be the last time any law student dares tease me about the inferiority of the female sex!"

"Blacks are inferior!" another student said when Elizabeth announced that she was about to go visit her cousins, the Smiths, in Peterboro. The Smith home had become famous as a station on the underground railroad. They hid runaway slaves and helped them escape to Canada, where slavery was not allowed. "Abolitionists are crazy fools!" the student went on, "and I'm amazed that Judge Cady is letting you go to Peterboro to be with them."

In fact, Elizabeth's father did *not* approve of abolition, but the Smiths were close relatives of Mrs. Cady. The Judge agreed to the visit, and Elizabeth arrived in Peterboro eager to learn more.

Elizabeth's cousin Libby came running out to greet her carriage. "Elizabeth, I'm so glad you're here. So much is going on! We have a houseful of guests and they're wonderful company."

After her many debates with the law students at home, Elizabeth felt confident about talking with these people as they discussed the political issues of the day. Many young men gave her an extra look when she was introduced, and at dinner one night all eyes turned to her when she was asked her father's opinion about slavery.

"He is a Judge who supports the law," she said, "and slavery is legal."

Later, cousin Gerrit Smith took Elizabeth aside. "Can you keep a secret?" he asked.

"Yes," answered Elizabeth.

"Then follow me," he said, leading her upstairs to the third floor.

There in a large room sat a beautiful slave girl named Harriet. About eighteen years old, she had run away from her master, who was visiting in Syracuse. The Smiths were going to help her make her way to Canada, where she would be free.

"I don't know where my mother and father are," she said. "I was taken from them and sold at a slave market in New Orleans. The man who bought me has used me very badly. I have to get away!"

Elizabeth saw the fear and desperation in Harriet's dark eyes. She looked much older than her eighteen years.

Elizabeth had always believed black people were as good as whites. Peter had been one of her most beloved childhood companions. But she hadn't known what to think about abolition, which meant to oppose laws which allowed white men to own black slaves.

She said to Gerrit after they went downstairs, "Thank you for letting me meet Harriet. Now that I've heard her story, I have no doubts about abolition. Slavery is wrong, and any law allowing slavery is wrong!"

The next day the Syracuse marshals and Harriet's master knocked at the Smiths' door and said loudly, "We demand to search this house. We think you are hiding a runaway slave!"

Mr. Smith calmly invited them all in. "Feel free to search anywhere you like, but I'm sure you'll see no slave is here. And please, do stay and join us for dinner. We were just about to sit down to eat."

Elizabeth sighed with relief when the marshals did not go upstairs. They assumed Harriet must not be there, for why else would Mr. Smith so willingly offer to let them search? They ate a big meal together, talking pleasantly all the while.

Later, the news came. While the Smiths had been graciously entertaining the marshals, Harriet had crossed Lake Ontario. "She is now safe in Canada!" said Elizabeth, and everyone in the Smith household felt better that night, knowing that at least one more girl could now call her life her own.

Henry
and a Honeymoon

I n autumn in New York State the oaks and maples undergo a glorious transformation, their leaves changing from shades of green to bright red, yellow and orange. Elizabeth, too, changed during the fall of 1839.

She often met famous abolitionists who stayed with the Smiths in Peterboro, but that fall the Smith household was expecting a special visitor—Henry B. Stanton, the man everyone said was the best speaker of them all on the subject of abolition. He could make his listeners laugh or cry, as he wished, and he certainly was able to convince an audience that slavery was wrong.

When Stanton's carriage arrived in Peterboro, Elizabeth saw that he was accompanied by a beautiful woman. As the couple drove up, someone whispered to Elizabeth, "Miss Stewart and Mr. Stanton are engaged to be married." Miss Stewart was as pretty to look at as Henry Stanton was handsome. As the days wore on during Henry's visit at the Smiths', Henry and Elizabeth often ended up deep in conversation about slavery, about politics, about education, about any and everything. Then one day to Elizabeth's surprise, Miss Stewart left Peterboro to go marry Luther Marsh! So, Henry was free after all!

Elizabeth was usually self-confident, but Henry's manner one Indian summer morning made her feel strangely uneasy. Henry asked, "Would you like to go horseback riding with me today? For once I don't have any lectures to give, and I can think of no nicer way to spend the day than with you."

Elizabeth was not sure if it was just the warm weather that made her cheeks flush, or if it was the fond expression on Henry's face when he looked at her. She nervously changed into her riding clothes, and she and Henry set off. Elizabeth sensed that something was on his mind as they trotted and galloped over the rolling hills, but it was not until they had almost gotten back to the Smiths' that he finally spoke up. Henry said, "I've been a bachelor for thirty-four years because I've never met a woman before as intelligent, kind and brave as you are. You would make me the happiest man in the world if you say you'll be my wife." Elizabeth's heart nearly burst with joy, and without hesitating, she answered, "yes." Their future together looked as bright as the colorful leaves on the trees around them.

But just as those leaves fade and die when winter comes, so too did Elizabeth and Henry's dreams, for Judge Cady refused to allow them to marry.

"Henry Stanton is an abolitionist who helps slaves run away from their owners," Judge Cady said. "That means Stanton breaks the law, and no daughter of mine is going to marry a lawbreaker!" He wanted Elizabeth to marry any of Johnstown's proper young men, but instead she had chosen a reformer, a troublemaker who challenged the laws which Judge Cady worked to uphold. "How could you even think such a man would provide well for you?" he argued. "You must not marry him!"

Elizabeth loved her father, but she loved Henry, too. As had happened many times before, her father was saying *no*, but her heart was saying *yes*. In despair, she called off the engagement. But Henry kept writing long letters begging her to reconsider. Also, he told Elizabeth about his plans to go to London as a U. S. Representative to the 1840 World Anti-Slavery Convention. His trip would last eight months.

Elizabeth couldn't bear the idea of such a long separation. She decided to go ahead and marry Henry in spite of her father's opposition. Secretly, Elizabeth and Henry planned to elope. Then they would travel to Europe together on their honeymoon.

On May 1, 1840, Elizabeth and Henry joined their lives in a simple ceremony. The word *obey*, over the minister's objections, was left out of the marriage vows. Independent as always, Elizabeth said, "I will not promise to obey Henry, but I will gladly promise to be an equal partner to him." And she did.

The newlyweds boarded the steamer *Montreal*, on May 12th, bound for England. They talked excitedly about their future together, until they were joined by James Birney. He was the most important man in the Liberty party, of which Henry was a member. Birney was also to be a representative at the convention, and he wanted to discuss anti-slavery issues with Henry. Elizbeth was eager to talk about the ideas too, but Birney found her open manner unladylike. He even scolded her for being so familiar with her husband in public. "Mrs. Stanton," Birney said, "it is really quite improper for a woman to address her husband by his first name in public. You should learn to restrain yourself and call him Mr. Stanton." Elizabeth, however, had just married the man she loved, and she was in no mood to restrain herself with Henry!

Elizabeth's love of adventure was as strong as ever. One fairly calm afternoon far out at sea, she asked the Captain, "Won't you please hoist me in the chair up the masthead? I've seen some of the men go up, and I want to see the view from up there too!"

James Birney couldn't believe his ears. He took Henry aside and said, "You can't let her do that! No proper wife does such things!"

Elizabeth guessed what Birney might be saying, so she quickly jumped into the chair, and the ship's crew hoisted her up.

What a view from the highest lookout on the ship! Henry and Birney watched Elizabeth silhouetted against the pale blue sky. Her bonnet blew off, but she waved delightedly anyway to the men below. How vast was the ocean, with America so far to the west it was out of sight, and Europe so far to the east it too was out of sight.

"What tiny creatures we are," thought Elizabeth. From way up on the mast, she marveled at the figures below. The people on deck seemed all the same, their differences in size, shape and color no longer noticeable. "Truly we are all equal in God's eyes, too—men, women, black or white," she thought.

James Birney's thoughts, however, were not about equality. He exclaimed to Elizabeth when she came down, "How unladylike of you to go up there!" He stalked off, and Elizabeth and Henry looked at each other. Elizabeth worried to herself, "What will Henry think? Am I so terribly improper?" But her fears ended when he smiled and then burst into a hearty laugh. Oh, what happiness! They were free, and at their voyage's end they were to help others become free, too. Her smile glowed like the sun sparkling on the ocean. However, a few white caps on the surface of the sea hinted that the upcoming convention might not bring such smooth sailing.

In England and Europe

"Will the meeting please come to order?" The British gentleman pounded the gavel on the podium, and slowly the excited crowd quieted down.

The opening session of the 1840 World Anti-Slavery Convention was beginning, but Elizabeth and the other women were not on the convention floor. Neither wives of convention members nor female delegates sent by their anti-slavery societies were being allowed to participate. They were hidden in a gallery barely within earshot of the proceedings.

"This is unbearable," Elizabeth whispered through clenched teeth to Lucretia Mott, her new friend.

Lucretia, twenty-two years older than Elizabeth and the most famous of the women there, was a Quaker who had learned to take everything calmly, be it good or bad. She looked straight ahead.

Meanwhile, James Birney was addressing the convention. He said, "Women do not belong here at a meeting about slavery. It is a woman's place to obey her husband, not to be speaking in public as if his equal!"

A clergyman jumped to his feet amid the men's applause. "The Holy Scriptures define the sphere of womankind, and we who are God-fearing know that sphere is *not* at a meeting hall debating with gentlemen!"

The women, not allowed to be seated in the hall, to be convention members, or to speak, squirmed in their chairs and eyed each other with frustration. "How dare these men who claim to oppose injustice toward blacks openly support injustice toward women?" Elizabeth asked herself.

During most of the debate, Henry remained silent, listening thoughtfully in his seat next to Birney. Although she understood that Henry was afraid of offending Birney, the most powerful man in the Liberty Party, still Elizabeth kept waiting for her new husband to stand and defend the women's right to join the convention. Finally Henry spoke up, but it was only after it was clear that those who opposed the women were in the majority. He said, "With all due respect to my colleague, Mr. Birney, I beg to differ with him in this matter. I think it only fair and right that we admit the women, equally, as delegates." Elizabeth tried to smile, but everyone knew most of the representatives had already made up their minds. Only William Lloyd Garrison and a few other American men applauded. When the votes were counted, the women had lost. They could stay and listen from their distant seats, but they could not participate.

"We've traveled over 3,000 miles to attend this convention!" said Emily Winslow, a famous abolitionist from Boston. The many other well-known women there all nodded, feeling both angry and humiliated.

Most of the Americans were staying at the same hotel, a lodging on Queen Street. That night at dinner, James Birney sat at a small table near the Stantons. Elizabeth challenged his views on women's inferiority, and the other rejected wives

and delegates joined in. The next day Birney decided to move to another hotel, where, he said, "My dinner will be more peaceful."

When the convention resumed, William Lloyd Garrison rose and said, "After battling for so many long years for the liberties of African slaves, I can take no part in a convention that strikes down the most sacred rights of all women." He walked to the back of the hall and joined the women in the gallery, silent like them for the remainder of the convention.

"Abolition is his life's work," thought Elizabeth, "and he's sacrificed his opportunity to participate in the World Convention, in order to support the equality of women. What a just and honorable man!"

After that day's session, Elizabeth walked back to Queen Street with Lucretia Mott. Arm in arm, they talked about the noble gesture Garrison had made.

"Yet very few men are like Garrison," said Elizabeth, and Lucretia agreed. Overhearing them, a few of the other women hurried to catch up. Then they all started walking more slowly, but talking more quickly. "It is about time some demand was made for new liberties for women!" they all said.

During the twelve days the convention lasted, they listened to the men in silence. But Elizabeth's mind was spinning. Whenever she could be in Lucretia Mott's company, she sought her out. They talked about women's rights and changes that needed to be made. "We'll hold a convention and form an organization for women's rights," they promised each other, "as soon as we get home."

Excited about Lucretia's ideas, Elizabeth bid her a fond farewell when she and Henry left London. It was not surprising to Elizabeth when James Birney later remarked to Henry, "I disapprove of that Quaker woman, Lucretia Mott." "Hmph," thought Elizabeth to herself. "I know Lucretia disapproves of you, too, but she'd be much too polite to say so behind your back!"

Henry, Elizabeth and many of the other Americans crossed the English Channel and journeyed to Paris, taking a month to enjoy the sights. Elizabeth's French, though excellent when she was at Mrs. Willard's Seminary, unfortunately was quite forgotten.

One evening when she wanted a light snack consisting of a small piece of cake, she asked the porter for it, using the best French she could remember. Everyone in the American party was shocked when the porter finally returned, a full hour later, and handed Elizabeth a huge chunk of steaming, broiled meat. Given no silverware or plate, she just stared at the greasy sweetbreads. "I think I'd better find an interpreter from now on," said Elizabeth with a smile, while roars of laughter filled the room.

Henry had been invited to lecture throughout England, Scotland and Ireland, so he and Elizabeth returned to the British Isles for a tour to last several months. His speeches were very well received, and the Stantons made many new friends.

In Scotland one day, when Henry had a little time away from his busy lecture schedule, he and Elizabeth took a sailboat ride around Loch Lomond. They so enjoyed the outdoor air that they decided to go hiking the very next morning.

"Today we shall climb Ben Nevis," said Henry to their hotel keeper at breakfast.

"Oh, do take a guide with you," he said. "The mountain is much more rugged than it looks from here, and there's no clear trail."

"We are both excellent walkers," said Henry, "and we'll manage it just as we would a hill back in New York State. We'll return at noon for dinner."

The hotel keeper shook his head, but Henry and Elizabeth went on their way. "He has no idea what good strong hikers we are!" they thought.

But they hadn't gone very far before they realized that their experience on New York's hills was no match for the Scottish mountain covered by rocks, steep irregular cliffs, and cold springs.

Panting and perspiring as she climbed, Elizabeth thought, "I'm not about to let Henry know I'm exhausted already."

Leading the way, Henry thought the exact same thing.

However, they exchanged enthusiastic comments and continued, hoping for a gorgeous view and an hour's rest when they reached the top. Six hours later they finally scrambled to the summit, but the cold wind made staying there impossible for more than a few moments.

"It's beautiful below, isn't it?" said Elizabeth, shivering as she briefly surveyed the view.

"Yes, spectacular," answered Henry. "But I think we best head down, so nightfall doesn't catch us on the mountainside."

Cold, hungry and very tired, they started back. Soon a chill Scottish mist surrounded them. An owl hooted, surprised to hear human voices in the twilight.

"Look, Henry, I see a trail over there!" called Elizabeth, trying not to let him hear the anxiety in her voice.

But the trail lasted only a few yards before it disappeared in the dense heather. They resumed their slipping and sliding down the rough hillside.

"What's that I hear?" asked Elizabeth nervously, and they stood still to listen, their hearts pounding.

"It's a dog barking," said Henry, and then from out of the fog a dog appeared, followed by a young man.

"I'm the guide from the hotel. We thought I might find you still up here," he said cheerfully.

Feeling much more humble than when they had begun, Henry and Elizabeth followed the guide back, as darkness fell. A sense of relief seemed to warm them, and all they could think of was how hungry they were after 12 hours without a bite to eat. At the hotel, their host had thoughtfully prepared a late meal for them, and they ate it so eagerly they hardly took time to speak.

The next month Henry and Elizabeth traveled to Ireland. They were saddened by the poverty there and knew that their gifts to the many poor people could do little to help them for very long. Gloomy fall weather added to their feeling of depression, and by November their thoughts turned to America.

After eighteen days at sea on the new steamship *Sirius*, they docked in Boston. A train took them to New York City the day before Christmas. Elizabeth smiled happily as her sister Harriet, her husband and two children greeted them. She said, "How wonderful it is to be home again!"

Motherhood

"How can we get back to Johnstown in all this snow?" Elizabeth wondered aloud. Her sister Harriet said, "Why, the most beautiful way—a sleigh ride!"

After the holidays Elizabeth and Henry bundled up, bid goodbye to Harriet and her family in New York City, and climbed into a big sleigh drawn by a team of four strong horses. Gliding behind the swift bays, they traveled up the lovely snow-covered Hudson River Valley.

As they passed the beautiful scenery, Elizabeth found herself worrying. She remembered all too well how strongly Judge Cady had opposed the idea of her marrying an abolitionist. "How will father feel about Henry now?" she asked herself.

"Hello, my dear daughter," said Judge Cady warmly as Elizabeth and Henry entered the big familiar house in Johnstown. "Greetings, Henry. It's good to see you back safe from your long trip."

Elizabeth smiled with relief. Not only did her father forgive them for marrying against his wishes, but before long he even invited Henry to join his office, to study the law. So they settled into a comfortable life in Johnstown for the three years it would take Henry to prepare for the bar exam and be admitted into the legal profession.

As the pleasant months passed, Elizabeth noticed a change in herself. Her appetite and her waistline were growing. "Yes," she announced, "we're going to have a baby!"

While Henry studied law books, Elizabeth studied baby books. But most of the information in them, she discovered, was very old and not very sensible. "We're not going to raise our baby in old-fashioned ways," she said, and Henry knew she meant it.

To Elizabeth, the months seemed to pass slowly. She was impatient to bring a new life into the world. Finally, the baby arrived. Beaming with pride, yet feeling sad that Henry was away on business at the time, Elizabeth showed the baby to her family: "It's a boy! He's doing fine, and so am I. His name is Daniel, Neil for short."

A few weeks later, Elizabeth said, "The healthiest part of this baby is his lungs!" His cries could be heard throughout the house. "I wonder if that nanny has gone back to her old ways again." Elizabeth hurried up to the baby's room and found that, sure enough, the nanny had wrapped the baby's body in bandages so tight he couldn't move.

"How many times must I tell you those bandages are not good for little Neil?" Elizabeth asked impatiently. "Give me even one good reason for imprisoning him so."

"Why, Ma'am, his tiny bones aren't strong yet, and they'll all fall apart if he isn't wrapped together good and tight. All the books says so."

Frowning, Elizabeth answered, "That is a ridiculous superstition. Puppies and colts don't fall apart, yet their bones are left free to develop. I truly doubt that humans are not capable of natural growth."

She unwrapped the bandages, and Neil's cries softened and then stopped. "And we must open this window," said Elizabeth.

"But the evils will enter and poison him!" the worried nanny protested.

"No," said Elizabeth. "The sunshine and fresh air will be good for him, much better than the stuffiness of this room."

One by one, Elizabeth broke all the old rules of infant care, and to the nanny's amazement, the baby grew strong and healthy.

"The old ways aren't always the best ways," said Elizabeth one evening during dinner, "and books aren't always right."

Judge Cady chuckled. "At least now you're not about to cut up the baby books with your scissors as you threatened to do to my law books when you were a child!" He retold the story of young Elizabeth's intention to "cut out those mean laws," and everyone laughed at the memory. Elizabeth smiled, too, but she still had not forgotten her frustration about the injustices to women, nor her promise to change unfair laws. But at that moment the baby woke up and demonstrated that his lungs were still in fine shape.

Elizabeth stood up. "I think the baby's heard us at the dinner table and wants to let us know that he's hungry too." Off she went to feed her little son.

In 1843 Henry completed his studies with Judge Cady. He and Elizabeth moved to Boston where he began his career as a lawyer. What excitement they found there! Anti-slavery lectures were given often, and heated debates always followed. Elizabeth attended all of them, and she renewed her friendships with many of the abolitionsists, including William Lloyd Garrison, the man who had so nobly renounced the World Anti-Slavery Convention for rejecting women.

Before long, little Neil had a baby brother, named after his father. Judge Cady gave the growing family a house in nearby Chelsea, overlooking the Back Bay. Reformers and lecturers often gathered there to discuss new ideas. Elizabeth loved the stimulating life, and her happiness was marred only when Henry made political trips away from Boston. Elizabeth devoted herself to her sons; in 1845 another boy, Gerrit, was born, named after Elizabeth's cousin in Peterboro.

After several winters in Boston, Henry's lungs began to suffer from the damp weather. His career in the Liberty Party was not as successful as he had hoped, and he needed a change. In 1847 Judge Cady offered them a house in the small village of Seneca Falls, in upstate New York, and they accepted.

The new home for the Stanton family, a frame structure on Washington Street, needed a great deal of repair and restoration, and Elizabeth supervised the work. At first she enjoyed managing the busy household, but it wasn't long before Henry left on business and political trips and Elizabeth found herself alone and bored with the demands of three small children. Although she had servants to help, they were badly trained and unreliable. Elizabeth's duties as an isolated rural housewife seemed unending and dull, and she sorely missed the company of well-educated adults. She said to herself, "I'm suffering from mental hunger."

Elizabeth's nearest neighbors were poor Irish immigrants. Remembering the terrible poverty she'd seen in Ireland, she tried to help them, and eventually she became their guide in everything from baby care to legal matters to family arguments.

One night just after Elizabeth put Neil, Henry, Jr. and Gerrit to bed, she heard a soft knock at the door. It was little Timothy, one of the neighbor children. "Please, come quick, Mrs. Stanton. My Daddy's been drinking and I'm afraid he's going to hurt my mother!"

Throwing a shawl over her shoulders and calling to the servant to attend to her children's needs while she was gone, Elizabeth hurried after Timothy. The lane was muddy and the night was dark. "I hope Mrs. O'Connell is all right," she worried as she neared the small frame house.

Timothy opened the door for her, and his parents, surprised, both stared at Elizabeth. Patrick O'Connell, the father, held a whiskey bottle in one hand and an iron frying pan in the other. His pregnant wife was huddled behind the stove, trying to shield herself.

Elizabeth marched into the room, her blue eyes glaring with anger. "Put that skillet down, you fool!" she commanded. The strength and determination in her voice convinced the drunken man to obey. Timothy ran over to his mother. Anxiously, Elizabeth asked, "Kathleen, are you all right?"

"Yes, thank you, Mrs. Stanton. Just a bit shaken, that's all." She patted her unborn baby and sighed.

Elizabeth turned to Mr. O'Connell. "Tonight, Patrick, you are to sleep out in the barn. If you find the straw uncomfortable, then while you lie there I want you to think about the goodness of your wife, your son, and your child yet to be born." She grabbed the whiskey bottle, half empty, and threw the rest out. "Timothy, you and your mother get a good night's rest. You certainly deserve it."

Elizabeth walked slowly back to her home, deep in thought. "He'll be better for a few weeks, but I know he'll be drinking again. Why must women be so helpless if their husbands go bad?"

Baby Gerrit's cries greeted her as she entered her house shortly before midnight, so she went to his room to nurse him. "Truly a mother's job is unending," she thought, as little Henry and Neil, awakened by Gerrit's crying, joined them, each wanting attention for himself, too.

The First Women's Rights Convention

I n 1848 Elizabeth received a letter from Jane Hunt: "Please join us July 13 in Waterloo. Many interesting Quakers will be there, including dear Lucretia Mott, visiting from Philadelphia."

"Yes, I will be there," said Elizabeth. She remembered Lucretia well from their discussions in London during the World Anti-Slavery convention. She was eager to talk with her again.

"It's been so long since we've seen you," the women exclaimed as Elizabeth entered. "Please tell us about your family and your new life in Seneca Falls."

Elizabeth poured out her story. She talked about her adorable sons, but she also found herself telling about the many injustices she had felt and seen around her. The other wives and mothers knew exactly what Elizabeth meant when she said she felt trapped in tiny Seneca Falls minding the children and household, while Henry was free to travel and return at his convenience. Elizabeth also described the lives of the women she had seen who were mistreated by their drunken husbands. She recalled, from years before, the desperate women who had sought help from her father, yet the laws had given them none. She remembered and described her frustration when the boys back in Johnstown had gone off to college, a choice not available to girls. And she reminded them of the anger they had felt when women were excluded from the convention in London eight years before. She looked at Lucretia, who had been nodding her head in agreement, and asked, "Remember our promise to hold a women's rights convention when we got home from Europe?" Before Lucretia even had a chance to answer, everyone in the room was talking excitedly.

Then all eyes turned to Elizabeth. Her descriptions had moved them to want to act, and they looked to her for direction. "I think we should hold a public meeting for protest and discussion!" she said, and the planning began.

"There are so many injustices, we need to organize them—but how?" asked one woman. Elizabeth thought a moment, and then exclaimed, "I've got it! We'll use the document that every American man respects, and we'll show how it applies perfectly to women!"

"Which document? What do you mean?" they asked.

"The Declaration of Independence! 'We hold these truths to be self-evident that all men AND WOMEN are created equal. . . .' And instead of listing the American Colonies' grievances against England, we'll list women's grievances against American men!"

They reviewed the Declaration, substituting the word *women* for Colonies and *men* for King George of England. The most famous grievance from the 1776 Declaration was the call for "no taxation without representation." This applied to women's complaints, since women paid taxes on property they owned, but they were not allowed to vote for any representatives to government.

"Who will chair the convention?" the nervous women asked each other. It was considered highly improper for a woman to speak in public, and none of them had any experience leading a meeting. Lucretia's husband James Mott volunteered to do it, but it was decided that Elizabeth would be the main speaker. A notice was put in the local newspaper announcing the convention, which was scheduled for July 19 and 20, 1848, at the Wesleyan Chapel in Seneca Falls.

The morning of July 19 was bright and sunny. On the way to the Chapel, Lucretia told Elizabeth, "Remember what I warned you, and don't be disappointed if the turnout is not large. This is a busy time for the farmers." Elizabeth nodded. She expected a small audience of women who were curious to see what a women's rights meeting would be about. To her amazement, however, the roads were jammed with people coming to the meeting, but the door of the Chapel was locked! No one could get in! Elizabeth took charge of the situation and had her nephew hoisted up into one of the church windows; he came around and opened the door, and the people streamed in. No one had dreamed so many

women would attend, and forty men were there too. Over three hundred people came—working women angered by their wages being much less than men's, Quakers, reformers, abolitionists, and even the famous former slave, Frederick Douglass.

At 11:00 James Mott called the session to order. When it was Elizabeth's turn to speak, her heart pounded so hard that she could barely stand. She felt like running away. "Am I brave enough to do this?" she asked herself. "I'm afraid my family will disown me." Elizabeth walked slowly to the podium and talked to the crowd. "Louder!" someone yelled. She said, "We have met here today to discuss our rights and wrongs, civil and political." While she read the women's *Declaration of Rights and Sentiments*, the butterflies in her stomach seemed stronger than her voice, but Elizabeth's words set the debate in motion. The first Women's Rights Convention in America was under way!

The next day Elizabeth excited the audience to action. All the resolutions for social change were approved unanimously. Then Elizabeth suggested one more—the right to vote. Men laughed, women were shocked. Lucretia had warned Elizabeth that people would see such a radical demand as ridiculous. Even Henry had refused to attend when Elizabeth told him her plan to introduce such a resolution. The audience started shouting.

"How could women possibly vote? Voting booths are set up in barber shops and saloons, and women don't go there!" "Ha!" snorted another. "Will women take up cigar smoking too?" One lady said, "This is going too far. Everyone will laugh at us."

The debate went on, but Elizabeth would not change her mind. She knew that government makes laws, and only when women could vote for members of government would they have the power to change laws which treated them unfairly. Frederick Douglass agreed with Elizabeth and spoke in favor of her resolution. As a black man, he also did not have the right to vote, and he knew how important that right was. After his speech, the resolution was voted on by the convention. "Did it pass?" Elizabeth asked. "Yes, just barely," was the reply.

One hundred people, including Elizabeth's sister Harriet, signed their names to the resolutions. When Judge Cady heard about it, he rushed to Seneca Falls.

"Elizabeth and Harriet, how could you do such a thing?" he roared. "This is disgraceful. Withdraw your names at once!" Harriet's husband demanded the same thing, and Harriet gave in. Elizabeth, however, would not. Her heart was heavy because men she loved did not approve of her actions, but she held her head high, for she knew her cause was right.

"Have you seen the afternoon's papers?" stormed Henry a few days later. "Your women's rights convention is the subject of jokes in newspapers across the country!" Only the anti-slavery papers supported the new movement. The others said, "It's the end of motherhood!" and "Goodbye family!" People who had attended the convention were scorned by their friends, and many who had signed the resolutions withdrew their names. Only the most courageous held firm.

But on that July day when Elizabeth inspired that handful of women to organize the very first convention, she ignited a spark that would not be put out. Another convention was scheduled in Rochester two weeks later. Soon more were planned, in other states as well, and the Women's Rights Movement in America had begun!

"But Father, You Told Me To!"

The demands of motherhood kept Elizabeth very busy during the first few years after the Convention, but one winter afternoon in 1851 she heard more than the usual commotion from her sons downstairs. "Look! Look! What a funny skirt!" the boys yelled, and Elizabeth glanced out the window to see her favorite cousin, Libby Smith Miller, walking up to the Stanton home. Instead of wearing the conventional long flowing dress with its big petticoats, Libby had on full trousers. When most women crossed the muddy road that led to the house, they had to lift heavy skirts to keep the hems from dragging. Libby, in contrast, moved quickly and easily, with both hands swinging freely. "What a wonderful idea!" thought Elizabeth.

The new style soon came to be known as "bloomers," because Amelia Bloomer liked Libby's outfit so much that she advertised it in her newspaper. "The old heavy dresses seem like prisons by comparison," said Elizabeth when she tried the bloomer outfit. It consisted of a pair of loose fitting trousers covered by a knee-length skirt.

But women's convenience and freedom of motion were of no concern to most people when they saw the new dress. As Elizabeth and Libby passed by, men pointed, women laughed and little boys chanted,

> Heigh! Ho! In rain and snow,
> The bloomer now is all the go.
> Twenty tailors take the stitches,
> Twenty women wear the breeches.

Libby said to Elizabeth, "I wish people wouldn't get so upset about such a simple improvement in dress!" Elizabeth answered, "I agree. These clothes are comfortable and the most practical I've ever worn. If only people weren't so closed minded. . . ." They hurried on, trying to ignore the criticism.

In the spring of 1851 Elizabeth was pleased to learn that her old friend William Lloyd Garrison had called an anti-slavery meeting in Seneca Falls. He and his colleague George Thompson accepted her invitation to be house guests at the Stantons.' Walking home after the rally, Elizabeth and her two guests saw a pair of women approach—Mrs. Amelia Bloomer and Miss Susan B. Anthony. Introductions were exchanged, but Elizabeth's thoughts were on Neil, Henry, Gerrit and little Theodore, the youngest addition to the family. "I'm so sorry," Elizabeth said, "but I'm afraid we really must hurry along. My sons, I suspect, may be up to their usual mischief, and I've already been away much of the afternoon."

Elizabeth didn't realize she'd just met the woman who was to become her very best friend and most loyal co-worker! Unaware of the importance Susan B. Anthony would soon have, Elizabeth was preoccupied with worries about her children. "I hope the nanny has been minding them well," she said, excusing herself so she could hurry along home.

Elizabeth's fears about the nanny were later confirmed. One day when she crossed the Seneca River on her way home to Washington Street, Elizabeth glanced down at the water below and saw what no mother should ever have to see. Eighteen-month-old Theo had been tossed into the water, and Henry and some of his friends were watching him, and laughing, as he splashed about! Fortunately Elizabeth was wearing bloomers, and even though she was seven months' pregnant, she was able to run down the bank and grab the baby, who was blue from the cold. A string of corks dangled from his arms.

"What is the meaning of this?" she demanded of Henry and his friends.

"It's an experiment. Corks float, so we decided to invent a cork life preserver, and we were just trying it out on Theodore."

The inventor was advised to be a little less bold experimenting on his youngest brother, and the nanny was scolded for failing to supervise the children more closely. The subject of the experiment, Theodore, recovered promptly from his very unusual "baptism."

On October 20, 1852, Elizabeth had yet another baby, this time a girl. Happily, Elizabeth named her first daughter Margaret after her mother and sister.

Caring for the four boys and a new baby was made easier due to the freedom Elizabeth had to move about when she wore bloomers. However, most people still considered the outfit immodest and disapproved heartily of it. Elizabeth, like the other women, decided that when she spoke in public, she would return to wearing the traditional long skirts. Elizabeth said, "People are only looking at my costume and not listening to what I have to say. It is more important that our ideas be heard." Dress reform was the least important of the many issues on Elizabeth's mind.

She vividly remembered meeting Susan B. Anthony, who had impressed her as a quiet yet strong Quaker woman. Elizabeth and Susan's paths crossed again, and their friendship quickly grew. Susan was an organizer and a dedicated worker. Unmarried, she could devote her entire energy to reform.

"Aunt Susan," as Elizabeth's children soon called her, regularly came to Seneca Falls to encourage Elizabeth to write speeches and letters. Since Susan was free to travel, she often delivered the speeches that Elizabeth wrote. The two women made a perfect team in the growing battle for women's rights.

One day in 1854 when Susan was visiting, Elizabeth found herself barely listening to her friend's words. Instead, she paced the room nervously. The New York State Women's Rights Association had urged Elizabeth to speak directly to the lawmakers, saying to her, "On all accounts, you are the person to do it." Elizabeth asked Susan, "But can I do a good job? I'd be the first woman ever to address the State Legislature."

"You will write a brilliant speech!" Susan said. "This is a wonderful opportunity. At last the men in Albany will listen to us!"

Elizabeth took great care in preparing the speech. She stayed up late working on it, night after night, while the children slept. Susan contributed helpful ideas, too. Finally, it was ready.

Elizabeth knew that Henry was upset by her radical plan to speak, but still she was determined to present the case for women's rights directly to the lawmakers. When she stopped in Johnstown at the Cady family home on her way to Albany,

Elizabeth found that her father, too, was angry. He had read in the newspapers about her intentions, and he demanded she discuss the matter with him before she went ahead with it.

Late one evening, Elizabeth entered the Judge's office so she could read him her speech. "I feel just like I did when I was a child, sent here for being naughty!" she thought as she sat down in the big familiar chair. Elizabeth knew her father strongly disapproved of the women's rights movement, and especially her active part in it. She dreaded displeasing him yet another time.

She began reading the speech to him. Frowning, he listened. She described the pitiful conditions of widows and the harsh laws that made life so difficult for women. Sincerity of feeling showed in her voice, and when Elizabeth glanced up, she saw tears in her father's eyes. "At last," she thought, "he will understand why I believe in this cause."

After Elizabeth finished reading, Judge Cady sat silent, deep in thought. Nervously, she waited for him to say something.

He finally spoke. "Surely you have had a happy life. How can you feel so keenly the wrongs against women? Where did you learn this lesson?"

"I learned it here, in your office, when I was a child listening to the complaints women made to you."

Judge Cady sighed.

"And remember when I wanted to cut those mean laws out of your law books after Flora Campbell came to see you?"

He nodded.

"You told me, when I grew up, to go talk to the men in Albany who make the laws. And now that's what I'm going to do."

He stared at his grown daughter, now an able woman. He remembered years before, wishing his strong-willed little girl had been a boy. He sighed again, and looking at the speech, said, "If you must do this, let me help you do it well. You have made your points clear and strong, but I think I can find you even more cruel laws than those you have quoted."

He made several suggestions, and they worked together until one in the morning. In the finished speech, Elizabeth demanded that the Legislators give women the exact same rights that men had, such as the right to vote, to serve on juries, and to keep the money they earned, instead of having to give it all to their husbands.

Susan printed 20,000 copies of the speech and distributed them everywhere, and Elizabeth's fame as the most persuasive speaker in the struggle for women's rights grew. Newspapers criticized her ideas constantly, but they could not dare ignore her. Even the New York State Legislature had listened to her. But the laws remained unchanged, and Elizabeth knew that it would take much more than one strong speech to end injustice against women.

The Civil War and the Negro's Hour

" It passed!" Elizabeth said happily. Six years had gone by since she had given her first speech to the New York State legislature. During that time she and Susan had worked tirelessly—lecturing, writing articles and circulating petitions for women's rights. In 1860 Elizabeth had addressed the Legislators in Albany again. A month after her speech, the Earnings Bill was finally passed giving married women the right to keep their own property. "Widows like Flora Campbell will now have some protection," thought Elizabeth, "but we still don't have the vote!"

The loud voices of her growing sons, arguing in the hall, interrupted her thoughts.

"Stop fighting with each other!" she said. "We've all heard so much talk about war lately, we certainly don't need battles between brothers here in our own home!" The boys lowered their voices, and Elizabeth rocked baby Robert's cradle. Harriot, now four, skipped into the room, chased by her older sister Margaret.

"What a fine brood of seven healthy children I have!" said Elizabeth, smiling proudly. "I only wish the health of our nation was as good."

The last few years had not been easy. Dangerous tension had developed between the slave states in the South and the abolitionists in the North. The country seemed to be dividing in two over the slavery issue. When Elizabeth and Susan spoke at anti-slavery meetings, the crowds got so angry that yelling and fistfights often broke out. Many Northerners knew that to be against slavery meant to be against the South, and war seemed all too likely.

At an anti-slavery rally in Albany, Elizabeth and Susan sat nervously on the speakers' platform. Accustomed to the noisy crowds at the other anti-slavery meetings, Susan looked at the audience and said, surprised, "People are quiet for once!"

51

"I know why," said Elizabeth. "Look at the Mayor." Across his lap, he held a big gun which everyone in the crowd could see. That night, at least, people listened when Elizabeth compared black slaves and white women. "Custom and prejudice enslave us both!" she said.

Tensions between the North and South continued to grow, and on April 12, 1861, the first shots of the Civil War were fired at Fort Sumter. Three days later the newspapers announced: "President Lincoln Calls for Volunteers." The war was beginning.

Also beginning was a new era in Elizabeth's life.

For years Henry had been spending months away from Seneca Falls arguing for abolition with the politicians in Albany and Washington. He met many powerful men in the new Republican Party, and in 1862 they appointed him to a position in New York City. Excited, the Stanton family bid farewell to Seneca Falls and moved to New York.

"We women must do something to help the Union. Our nation's life is at stake," Elizabeth said to Susan after the Stantons had settled in their new home. Together they formed the Women's Loyal League, whose purpose was to nurse the sick and wounded, prepare food, make clothes, and collect signatures on petitions calling for an end to slavery.

"We want to help, too!" Elizabeth's children said, so they rolled up and labeled the petitions as they came in. From their office in New York City, Elizabeth and Susan sent hundreds of thousands of petitions to the President and Congress. Never before had so many people signed so many petitions!

One evening Henry glanced up from his newspaper and told Elizabeth, "Your Women's Loyal League is really making a difference. It's doing a wonderful service for the country."

"But Susan worries we women will be forgotten when the war ends," said Elizabeth. "She thinks we're making a mistake by devoting ourselves to anti-slavery and setting aside the issue of women's rights."

Henry answered, "Don't worry. Listen to what the *New York Tribune* says: 'The women of the Loyal League have shown great practical wisdom and great courage!' " He took a puff on his pipe. "When this war ends, and the slaves are free, women's patriotism will be remembered."

Indeed, women's patriotism may have been remembered, but it was not rewarded. After the Civil War and the abolition of slavery, both white and black women still lacked many freedoms.

In 1866 the vote was still limited to white men, so Elizabeth and Susan founded the American Equal Rights Association. They wanted all adults, no matter what race or sex, to have the rights of full citizenship, including the vote.

But the white men in power were reluctant even to allow black men to vote. "To allow all women to vote as well," they said, "that's asking too much!" Many men who had once supported women's suffrage, or women's right to vote, now said that black men should come first. Then it would be women's turn.

Elizabeth thought back to the 1840 World Anti-Slavery Convention over twenty-five years before. The men there who said they supported justice for blacks had not allowed women to participate. She remembered watching them in silence. She would not be silent now!

Elizabeth was told, "It is the Negro's hour. Black men come first, and you women must wait." She answered, "No. Women are not going to let you forget that we too deserve our rights."

Elizabeth decided to try something no other woman had ever dared. In 1866 she became a candidate for U. S. Congress. "Even though women are not allowed to vote," she said, "nothing in the Constitution says we are not allowed to run for political office."

As she expected, people were very shocked by the idea of a woman wanting to take part in national government, and Elizabeth realized she had no chance of being elected. However, she did succeed in bringing more public attention to the injustices against women. Increasing numbers of people listened to her ideas, and the women's rights movement continued to grow.

Campaigning
in Kansas

"**M**rs. Stanton, we need you and Miss Anthony to campaign for women in Kansas. Please come west!"

Elizabeth's mind raced as she read the invitation in 1867 from women's rights workers in that newly-created state. Kansas voters were to decide on two propositions in November, one extending the vote to women in the state, and one giving it to black men. The invitation said, "This is the first time any state has come this close to granting women suffrage. The excitement is tremendous!" How Elizabeth wanted to help. But, she thought, "What about my family? A speaking tour could last for months, and Margaret and Harriot and little Robert still need me at home."

That night after dinner she asked Henry what he thought. They both knew he regularly spent many months away from home, leaving the children and the management of the household all to Elizabeth.

He roared, "Do I want you to travel 1500 miles away? Do I want you to leave our home for months? Of course not!" He paced the floor for a long time, but then turned to Elizabeth and said in a gentle tone, "I know this trip is important to you. Amelia is a fine housekeeper, and the children adore her. Just as you have managed without me when I've been away, everyone will manage here so that you are free to go."

In July, Elizabeth and Susan boarded the train bound for Kansas. When they arrived in the state's large eastern cities, they were welcomed and cheered by the crowds. Encouraged, they separated, each setting off with high hopes to cover big sections of rural western Kansas.

Former Governor Charles Robinson offered to accompany Elizabeth, and they took turns driving a mule-drawn carriage across the vast prairies. There were almost no marked roads and few guideposts, and they often lost their way. Speaking engagements had been scheduled very close together, and they sometimes had to travel by night as well as day in order to reach their destinations on time.

One dark night, the Governor said, "Mrs. Stanton, there's a stream up ahead. Can you manage the reins while I get out and look for a spot to ford?"

"Certainly, Governor," she answered bravely. Her childhood adventures on horseback around Johnstown gave her confidence in handling the animals, but nothing in New York society had prepared her for river crossings by night! Luckily the Governor was wearing a white shirt, so she could just manage to see him in the darkness.

He waved for her to drive the carriage behind him. She urged the reluctant mules forward. On the surface, Elizabeth stayed quiet and calm, but inside she was afraid the Governor would stumble, a mule would slip, or the carriage would overturn. Slowly, unevenly, the mules started across the rocky stream. Elizabeth held the reins steady. Then, suddenly, the carriage jerked to a stop. The left wheel was wedged up against a boulder, and water surged around it. Elizabeth yelled at the mules, "Pull, pull hard!" and slapped the reins against their backs. They leapt forward, and the wheel scraped its way over the rock. Straining, the mules dragged the carriage the rest of the way across. Slowly, they climbed the slippery bank on the other side.

Elizabeth let the tired animals rest, and she breathed a sigh of relief. The Governor climbed back in and said to her, "You are very courageous, Mrs. Stanton." She was surprised her pounding heart hadn't given away how she actually felt, but all she said was, "Thank you, Governor. Your bravery set a good example."

Frontier life was rugged for everyone. Elizabeth thought, "It's a good thing these pioneers are used to seeing coarse and practical dress." That day she went directly to the lecture platform from the muddy seat of the carriage. This was no place for eastern fashions!

Generous farmers and ranchers offered Elizabeth their best lodging, which usually meant a hard bed she'd be expected to share—with hungry bedbugs! One night to escape them Elizabeth decided to sleep outside under the stars in the carriage she'd come to know so well. Just as she dozed off, she felt a big jolt.

"Who's there?" she cried out in surprise.

"Oink, grunt, gree," was her reply, and Elizabeth both laughed and groaned when she realized her pushy visitors were the farmer's long-nosed black pigs. They were energetically scratching fleas on the strong iron steps of the carriage. Elizabeth yelled at them in the most unfriendly language she'd ever used, and swung the whip at them, but those pigs were bothered more by the fleas than by Elizabeth's threats, and they kept on rubbing, all night long. After that sleepless night, Elizabeth said, "I think the bed bugs aren't so bad after all!"

Another night she accepted an invitation to stay in a small log cabin. Snugly in bed, she suddenly sat upright and exclaimed, "What was that?"

A family of mice had made a nest in her bedding, and the creatures had begun running over and around her to see what had upset their little home. The log cabin was small, and Elizabeth knew there was no other place for her to sleep. "Well," she thought, "the mice will probably care more about tending to the comforts of their own kind than making mischief with me." She determinedly closed her tired eyes, and thanks to her exhaustion from the day's long trip, she fell asleep. What frolic the mice enjoyed, she never knew—and tried not to guess.

Rough conditions were made up for by the warm response of the people who listened to her lectures. Curious folks would come from miles around to see and hear the famous suffragist from New York. Her reputation was growing.

But in spite of Elizabeth's and Susan's efforts, voting men from the East, with more money and political power, succeeded in defeating both propositions, and neither women nor black men won the vote in Kansas in 1867.

Elizabeth and Susan were disappointed, but not too discouraged. They realized how much hard work lay ahead. "We're going to need a lot more money to wage a successful campaign," said Elizabeth. When George Francis Train, a very wealthy politician, came out in favor of votes for women, Elizabeth and Susan accepted his help. He financed a women's rights newspaper, to be daringly called *The Revolution*. Susan was its publisher, Elizabeth the editor.

Radical ideas came pouring from Elizabeth's busy pen: equal pay to women who did the same work as men, but got lower wages for it; unions to help workers, and a political party that would unite women, blacks and laborers.

In 1870 most people thought these new ideas were crazy, and even Elizabeth's sister Tryphena wrote her, "Please, I beg you to give up this improper newspaper!" Lack of money finally did cause Susan and Elizabeth to sell *The Revolution,* but they never gave up their ideals.

"Most people's minds change very slowly," said Susan. "You're right," said Elizabeth with a sigh. She knew that many things would have to change before women would be accepted as equals. The vote alone would not solve all the problems.

"We must concentrate on one issue at a time," said Susan. Elizabeth frowned. She knew women needed rights on the job, in the courts, and in the home, as well as in government. But she looked at Susan and said aloud what she knew her friend was also thinking: "For right now, the most important thing is the vote for women!"

Women's Suffrage

" **Y**ou won't be able to make it," said the hotel keeper. "The train isn't running, the snow has blocked all the roads, and the winds are freezing cold!"

"Get the sleigh ready and I will try it!" said Elizabeth. She telegraphed ahead to say she'd be arriving as scheduled, and bundled up in a fur cloak, hood and veil.

At eight o'clock that night, the church bells in Maquoketa, Iowa, rang loud and long to announce Elizabeth's arrival. The well-heated lecture hall warmed her, and her speech excited this audience just as it had all the others on her tour.

For three weeks Elizabeth traveled forty to fifty miles a day in a horsedrawn sleigh. Undaunted by the winter storms, she lectured throughout northern Iowa. In Chicago she met two speakers, Mr. Bradlaugh and General Kilpatrick, touring on the same route.

"Where have you been?" she asked.

"Waiting here for the roads to clear. Travel is impossible," the men answered.

"It's not impossible for this woman!" she said, smiling proudly.

For twelve years Elizabeth traveled from every October to June giving speeches on women's rights, and her lecture fees helped pay for the children's schooling. Henry spent most of his time in New York City; home for Elizabeth was a big house she had bought in nearby Tenafly, New Jersey.

Education for women was very important to Elizabeth, and the unfairness of current laws made her especially upset one November in Michigan. "The University in Ann Arbor is one of the best in the country," said Elizabeth. "The money for it has come from the taxpayers, many of whom are women. But women are not allowed admission at the very University they've helped to finance!" Shortly thereafter, following the lead of Oberlin and a few other colleges, the University of Michigan did finally open its doors to women in 1870.

Remembering her own disappointment at not being able to attend Union College, Elizabeth was pleased when her daughters Margaret and Harriot went to Vassar College. Henry, Jr., Gerrit and Robert graduated from Columbia Law School, and Theo earned his M.A. at Cornell University.

In the summer of 1871 Elizabeth and Susan traveled together from New York to California, holding women's suffrage meetings in all the big cities on the way.

"While we're here," they said, "we must take time to see some of nature's wonders in the beautiful West." So with friends, Elizabeth and Susan took a carriage to Yosemite. They arranged ahead to have good horses waiting there to take them into Yosemite Valley. "Since I have become quite stout," said Elizabeth, "save the strongest horse for me."

When the carriage left them at the head of the trail, the horses were standing ready for the riders. The guide presented Elizabeth with a fat old nag whose back sloped so much it seemed as if he were walking downhill when he was really on level ground!

Susan mounted a neat Mexican pony and set off with the rest of the group. Elizabeth's horse was so broad she couldn't even reach the stirrups, and when he started down the trail, she felt as if she were about to fly over his head.

"I will walk down myself, rather than try to ride this ill-constructed beast!" she said.

"Walking this trail is impossible!" warned the guide.

Determined, Elizabeth got off the horse and started down. By this time the rest of the group had gone way ahead, so she slipped and slid her way down alone, on foot. The hot August sun beat down hard, and the loose rocks on the dusty path tumbled over the cliffs. Elizabeth's long skirt tore on the tree branches and her shoes gave up under the pressure. After four long hours, she finally reached the valley. Exhausted, she lay down on a patch of cool green grass and promptly fell sound asleep.

Before long the hotel sent a carriage to get her, and gratefully she climbed in, feeling very tired, stiff and hungry. She looked very different from her usual well-groomed appearance, what with her dirty clothes, dusty face and ruined shoes.

"We wondered what became of you! I'm so glad you finally made it!" said Susan, who had been waiting for Elizabeth at the hotel. "Wasn't the scenery magnificent?"

"I have no idea!" snorted Elizabeth. "I could only watch my feet on that narrow, slippery trail!"

Susan tried not to smile, but she couldn't help it, and burst out laughing at her bedraggled friend. Holding her sore sides, Elizabeth joined her.

Most of Elizabeth's adventures, however, were much more political than physical. One big event was the 4th of July celebration of 1876. The nation had reached its 100th birthday.

Elizabeth met Susan in Philadelphia where the anniversary would be held. They set up an office of their National Women's Suffrage Association and began work.

"We must present a bold speech on this occasion. One hundred years ago our nation was born in revolution when men demanded their rights. We women now must demand our rights!" said Elizabeth.

Working day and night, with the help of Susan and the other members of the Suffrage Association, Elizabeth prepared a new Declaration of Women's Rights. Then, as President of the Association, she wrote a letter to the man in charge of the 4th of July ceremonies. It said, "We ask your permission to read our Declaration of Rights immediately after the reading of the Declaration of Independence is finished." She also asked for seats on the speakers' platform and ended by saying, "Although these are small favors to ask as representatives of one-half the nation, yet we shall be under great obligation to you if granted."

The chairman sent six general admission tickets but denied them seats on the platform, time to speak, or a display area promised them months before in the exhibition hall. So Elizabeth, her old friend Lucretia Mott, and Matilda Joslyn Gage, another active women's rights worker, organized a separate convention to be held at the same time as the men's. The Women's Declaration would be heard!

On the 4th of July, Susan and five of the other members of the Suffrage Association first went to the men's celebration while Elizabeth began the proceedings at the women's convention. When Susan's group later entered the women's meeting, they reported what had happened:

"Using our six tickets, we found seats in the audience. Then after the Declaration of Independence was read, we walked forward and mounted the platform, acting as if we had been invited."

Elizabeth smiled, proud of her dear friend and the other brave workers.

Susan went on. "The chairman was taken by surprise. We presented him with our Declaration. As we left, hundreds of curious men in the audience called for copies of it, and we handed out all we had brought."

Everyone cheered, and Susan read the Declaration to the assembled women. She stood in front of the Liberty Bell which had these words on it: "Liberty to all the land and its inhabitants."

Elizabeth, now white-haired and no longer young, thought to herself, "For so many years we have worked for liberty for women! It's hard to believe that Lucretia and I first talked about holding a convention so long ago, back in 1840, when we met in London." Since then Elizabeth had raised seven children, lectured from coast to coast, written hundreds of articles and worked side by side with Susan for the goal still not achieved—women's suffrage.

In 1880 back at her home in Tenafly, Elizabeth began writing *The History of Women's Suffrage* with the help of Susan, as well as Matilda Gage. People from all over the country sent useful information. Within a year, volume one— all 871 pages of it—was published.

Anxiously reading the newspaper reviews of her first full book, Elizabeth exclaimed happily, "I can't believe it! They're praising *The History!*" She started in on volume two.

On November 2, 1881, election day, Elizabeth and Susan were hard at work as usual on *The History.* Elizabeth's mind had been drifting, and finally she looked up and said, "When the Republican carriage stops by looking for voters to take to the polls, I think I may just go down and vote! Would you like to come along with me?" Susan's eyes sparkled. "Of course," she said.

"The polls are set up in the hotel where I go to pay my taxes," Elizabeth told Susan as they rode in the carriage. When they arrived, they entered a room crowded with men.

Seeing them coming, the voting inspector grabbed the ballot box and held his hand over it protectively. "Oh, no,

Madam. Men only are allowed to vote!" he said to Elizabeth.

Handing him her ballot, Elizabeth answered, "I am a taxpaying citizen and I have the same right to vote as any man here." The other inspectors hid their faces behind their hats, and the man holding the ballot box threw her ballot on the floor.

The struggle to win women's suffrage was far from complete.

Three Generations: Elizabeth Cady Stanton with granddaughter Nora and daughter Harriot Stanton Blatch, 1892.

In Her Honor

"Elizabeth Cady Stanton, I'd like you to meet Elizabeth Cady Stanton," said Theodore, and Elizabeth gave her first grandchild a warm hug. Baby Elizabeth gurgled, and Theodore said, "Mother, she may be only three months old, but she's trying to tell us she already supports women's suffrage!" Everyone laughed, and the baby's bright blue eyes, amazingly like Elizabeth's, sparkled merrily.

Elizabeth spent the summer of 1882 in Europe visiting the families of her children Theodore and Harriot, who lived there. Henry stayed in New York City. When Susan crossed the Atlantic to join Elizabeth, they traveled in Europe and England. As America's two most famous women, they were warmly welcomed wherever they went.

Before long, back home, they resumed work on *The History of Women's Suffrage,* now into its third volume. "The more I think about our struggle to win the vote," said Elizabeth one day, "the clearer it seems to me that we must deal with the fact that religion has played a big part in our lack of freedom."

When Elizabeth presented this idea to the 1885 National Women's Suffrage Association Convention, the women were shocked and upset. In spite of Susan's support, the convention would pass only milder resolutions than the strong ones Elizabeth had proposed. For Elizabeth, there was nothing new about her ideas being called too radical. "I've heard that all my life!" she said.

As he grew older, Henry started spending less time in New York City, preferring the comforts of home with Elizabeth in Tenafly. One day not long after the stormy convention, Henry asked her, "Have you seen the latest issue of *The New Era?*"

"No, but I suppose they're criticizing my comments about religion," she said, frowning.

"Quite the opposite, my dear! It says you're to be honored on your 70th birthday at the New York meeting of the

Suffrage Association. And they want you to deliver a speech on the *Pleasures of Age.*"

Elizabeth smiled with surprise, and Henry said, after taking a slow puff on his pipe. "I suggest you don't mention your husband's rheumatism when you talk about the joy of maturity."

He settled back into his chair, and Elizabeth winked. Henry still looked very handsome, but indeed he was slowing down and becoming an old man. As for Elizabeth, her energy was still going strong. In spite of her plumpness, she was constantly active.

On the morning of November 12, 1885, the doorbell at the Stanton home rang constantly. The living room overflowed with birthday packages, letters, telegrams, flowers, baskets of fruit, gift books, pictures and silver. Elizabeth's heart, too, was overflowing. At the birthday celebration, Susan said to the crowd of admirers, "I never expect to know any joy in this world equal to that of going up and down the land engaging halls and circulating Mrs. Stanton's speeches. If I ever have had any inspiration, she has given it to me." Everyone cheered, and tears filled the eyes of many of the guests.

That winter Susan and Elizabeth once again devoted themselves to *The History,* completing the third and final volume in 1886. But Elizabeth's mind was still bubbling with ideas about women and religion. She said to her daughter Harriot, then visiting from England, "Many women have struggled to understand what the Scriptures really say about woman's true place in the world. I'm convinced that women have been fooled by many superstitions. We need to study the Bible and what's been written about it, and then interpret what we learn so women will understand." Harriot said, "I'd like to help," and so they began work.

Few people supported the project. "You'll offend everyone!" they warned. "No one will approve." Unfortunately, Harriot would have to leave soon, and with no other help, Elizabeth had to put the work aside, but she was determined that it would not be forgotten.

In late October, 1886, Harriot convinced her mother to return to Europe with her and her daughter Nora. With them in England that winter, Elizabeth received the cablegram announcing that at age 82, Henry had died. Elizabeth wrote in her diary, "The startling news comes as a terrible shock." Although they had spent much time apart, Henry was the only man she had ever loved—they had been married nearly fifty years.

Through the winter, Elizabeth mourned Henry's passing, but by springtime her spirit was restored and she journeyed to Paris to see her son Theodore. Following in his mother's footsteps, he too had written a book on women's rights, called *The Woman Question in Europe.* Elizabeth said, "I appreciate more than ever what each generation can do for the next one, by making the most of itself."

In the fall of 1887 Elizabeth went back to England to be with Harriot and little Nora. When not acting the part of devoted grandmother, she took advantage of her leisure time to read and write as much as she liked.

One day early in 1888 Harriot gave her mother a letter from "Aunt Susan" urging Elizabeth to return to America immediately to celebrate the fortieth anniversary of the first Women's Rights Convention. Elizabeth cabled back, "I am coming." She and Susan met in Washington, D. C. As had been the pattern for years, Susan asked Elizabeth to write a speech, and of course, she did.

Many women's rights groups joined together at the meetings Susan had scheduled. Elizabeth was named president of the new coalition, the International Council of Women. She spent the next few years writing speeches as well as visiting her grown children and getting to know all her grandchildren.

"But in the back of my mind," she told Susan, "I am still thinking about the *Woman's Bible* project. Several women came forward to help, and finally, in 1895, it was published.

"It's the work of Satan!" cried ministers. Newspapers in America, England, and Europe ran long articles about the shocking new book. But, so many copies were sold, three more editions had to be printed! It was a best seller.

People from all over the world wrote to Elizabeth asking for advice not only on religion, but on every issue of concern to women. She advised, "Let each woman do what seems right in her own eyes, provided she does not encroach on the rights of others." "Please tell us about yourself, too," women said, and Elizabeth began work on her autobiography, eventually published under the title *80 Years and More.*

"How can Elizabeth's 80th birthday be honored?" wondered her friends and admirers. "I know," said Susan. "The National Council of Women will hold a grand celebration for her in New York City."

Invitations referred to Elizabeth as "an inspiration, a queen among women." Hundreds of organizations joined in sponsoring the event, and six thousand cheering people welcomed the guest of honor. Very overweight, she walked with the help of a cane to the speaker's platform.

"I am terribly nervous," Elizabeth confided to Susan. Susan laughed. "Why should you be nervous? You've given hundreds of speeches, and usually to audiences who don't agree with many of our beliefs about women's rights."

Elizabeth answered, "That's right. I am much more accustomed to hearing criticism than praise!" But praise she heard, from both sides of the Atlantic, for her lifetime of work on behalf of women.

Elizabeth thought about her past. "I remember when our first convention in Seneca falls in 1848 was called 'a great mistake.' We were warned that we'd be laughed at, and indeed we were. But today, many such conventions are held throughout the country every year."

"I also remember when my speech to the New York State Legislature in 1860 was called 'a great mistake.' Yet today the public is thankful for the new laws that passed after I gave that speech."

"Some people today feel the *Woman's Bible* is 'a great mistake.' In time, I know that it, too, will be seen as a step forward. I repeat my demands for justice, liberty and equality for women in the church as well as the state!"

Truly, Elizabeth's spirit and courage never changed. Slowly, though, her physical health and eyesight began to fail, until she became totally blind. On October 25, 1902, she said to her physician, "I hope to be speeded on to heaven when I can no longer work." The very next day, in her sleep, she did speed on to heaven, leaving behind a world much brighter for her having been in it.

Afterword

T he memory of Elizabeth's courage helped the battle for women's suffrage to continue. Susan said, "Failure is impossible," but like her dear friend Elizabeth, she too died before American women won the vote.

Elizabeth's daughter Harriot Stanton Blatch became an important women's rights leader in the early 20th century. She returned to New York, determined to realize her mother's dream that all women should be able to vote as men's equals. In 1907 she founded the Equality League for Self-Supporting Women. Women made less than half the pay men earned, and worked for ten to twelve hours a day in terrible conditions. To them, the right to vote meant the possibility of electing people who would pass laws to protect them from cruel and unfair bosses. Harriot's League quickly enlisted thousands of members who held huge parades which attracted national attention.

By 1911, six western states had granted women suffrage—Wyoming (1890), Colorado (1893), Idaho (1896), Utah (1896), Washington (1910) and California (1911). But an amendment to the Constitution of the United States was needed in order to give all American women the right to vote. Carrie Chapman Catt, Anna Shaw and Alice Paul, as well as Harriot Stanton Blatch, all worked hard to achieve the goal. Angry women who felt frustrated by the many years of unsuccessful struggle, picketed, got arrested, and made daily newspaper headlines.

World War I brought even more women into the work force. They proved once again that women could handle responsibilities beyond the home. Relying on the goods supplied by the women who worked in the factories, the American armed forces returned victorious in 1919.

Even though World War I was over, American women's battle for the vote still remained to be won. In the summer of 1919 the U. S. Congress finally passed the Women's Suffrage

Amendment to the Federal Constitution, but it would not become law until at least 36 states also passed it. Nervously the suffragists worked for another year to persuade lawmakers across the country to support the amendment. Tennessee became the needed 36th state in a very close vote—49 to 47.

Finally, on August 26, 1920, the 19th amendment became the law of the land: "The right of citizens of the United States to vote shall not be denied or abridged by the United States or by any state on account of sex." Seventy-two years had passed since Elizabeth called for women's right to vote in 1848 at that very first convention held in the small Methodist Chapel in Seneca Falls, New York.

Elizabeth Cady Stanton knew that the vote was vital in the struggle for women's rights in America, but she realized it would not in itself guarantee women social, economic, religious and political equality with men. The ongoing feminist movement today shows that Stanton did not underestimate the power of tradition and prejudice, or women's determination to overcome them.

Acknowledgments

Anne R. Knight for the line art drawings.

Brigham Young University Photoarchives for the photograph of "Young Elizabeth."

Rhoda Barney Jenkins for the "Three Generations" photograph.

Carol Kammen and Corinne Guntzel for reading the manuscript.

About the Author

Born and raised in Rochester, New York, Martha E. Kendall graduated from the University of Michigan in 1969 and holds advanced degrees from Stanford University and San Jose State University in California. She currently teaches English and Women's Studies at San Jose City College.

Kendall has also written and produced a video and book entitled *Scenes of American Life* which explains American culture to immigrants and foreign students.

She and her husband Joe Weed, a professional musician, live in Los Gatos, California, with their two children, Jeff and Katie.

In this publication, the text was keyed and edited on a TRS-80 IV microcomputer and set on a Digitek 3000 in 11 point ITC Benquait Book with heads in matching 30 point bold.

Printed in PMS 470 on Tomohawk 80 lb. Cool White Text with matching cover.

A *quality* product, produced in New York State, by Heart of the Lakes Publishing, as a part of a continuing commitment to local and regional studies of the Empire State.